Contents

Going to the Dentist

Today I am going to the dentist.
So, I brush my teeth.

Here we are at the dentist's office.

His name is Dr. Singh.

In the Waiting Room

We meet the **receptionist.**

We can read or play
in the waiting room.

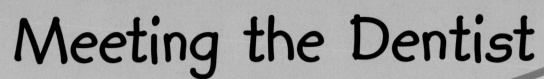

Meeting the Dentist

I meet Dr. Singh.
I sit in his big chair.

8

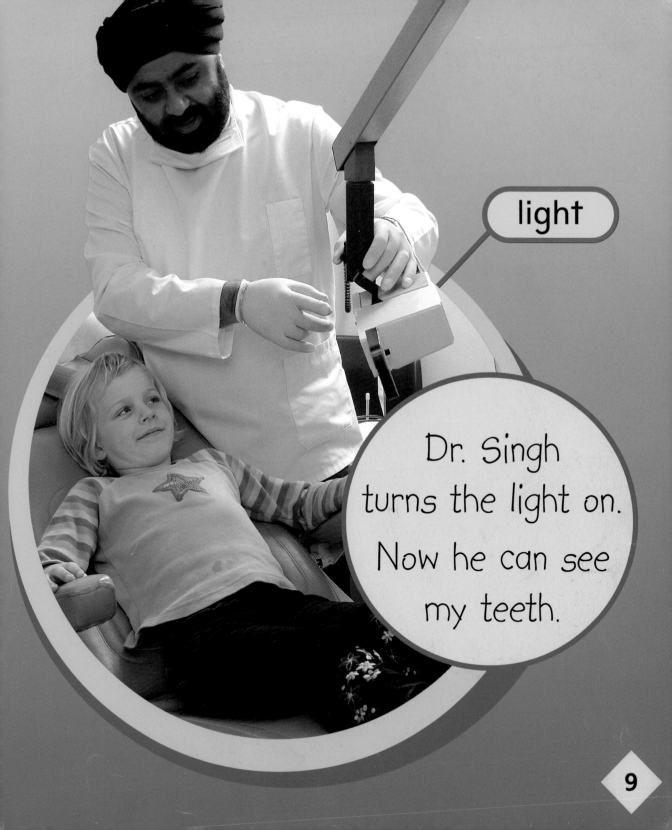

light

Dr. Singh turns the light on. Now he can see my teeth.

9

Getting Ready

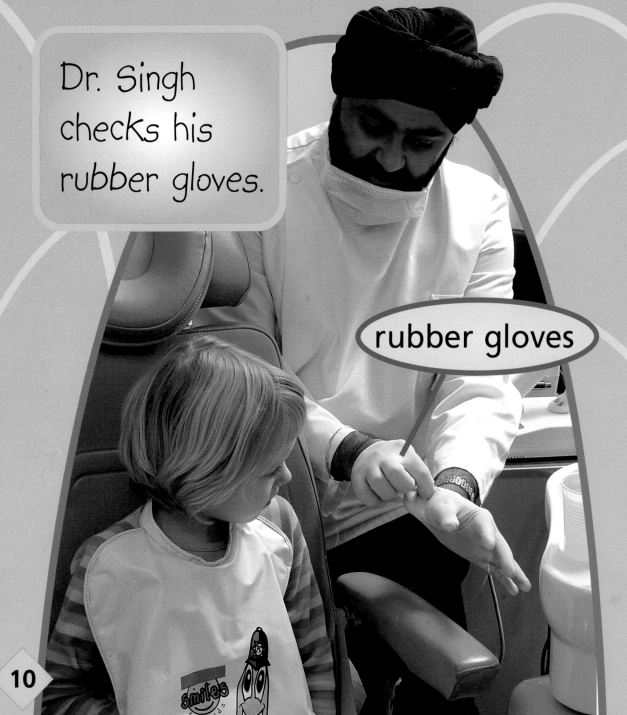

Dr. Singh checks his rubber gloves.

rubber gloves

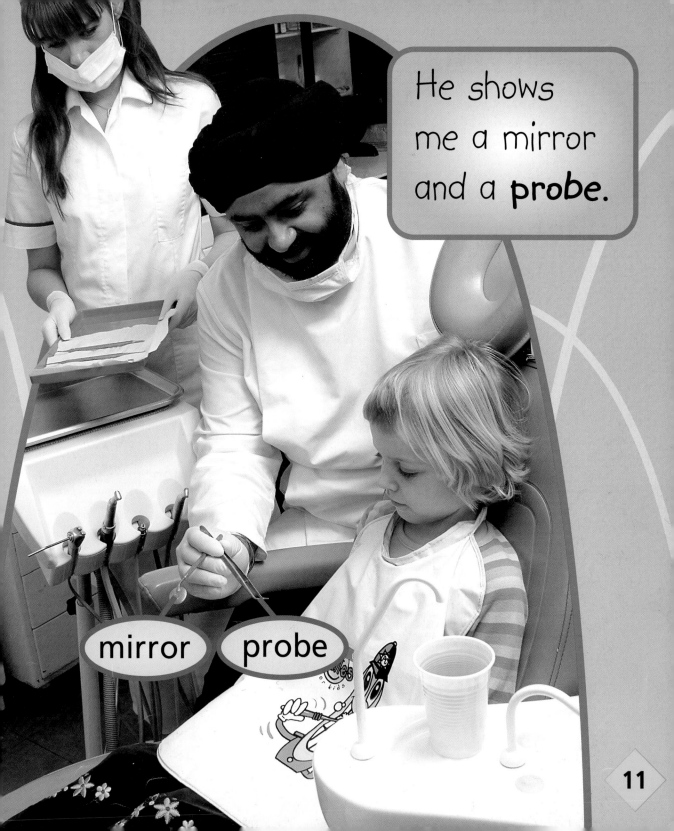

The Checkup

safety glasses

I wear **safety glasses.**

Dr. Singh looks at my teeth with the mirror.

He finds a **cavity** with the **probe**.
The **assistant** writes it in my **chart**.

Fixing Teeth

Dr. Singh fixes the **cavity.**

He says I may need braces.

Clean and Shiny

Dr. Singh cleans my teeth.

The electric toothbrush buzzes and tickles.

The **assistant** helps me rinse my mouth.
Now my teeth are clean and shiny.

Brushing My Teeth

Dr. Singh shows me how to brush my teeth.

Now I can brush my teeth the right way.

19

All Done!

The **assistant** helps me choose a sticker.

The **receptionist** gives me a new toothbrush.

21

Time to Go

I will eat good food to keep my teeth healthy.

Glossary

assistant   a person who helps in an office

braces   metal and plastic parts that a dentist puts on your teeth to make them straighter

cavity   a hole in a tooth

chart   papers that a dentist or doctor keeps that show how you are each time you visit

probe   metal tool that a dentist uses to check your teeth for cavities

receptionist   person who works in an office answering phones, meeting people, and making appointments

safety glasses   glasses that protect your eyes

Index